An aerial view of Bristol dating from the late 19th century

The New World

The New World was to play a major part in Bristol's fortunes. The city became the primary port of departure for 17th-century emigrants. Later, Bristol's ships transported a more sinister cargo: they brought the city sugar, tobacco, cocoa and rum, but in return carried thousands of slaves – almost 17,000 in 1725 alone – from the west coast of Africa to America via Bristol. Some people in Bristol, and particularly the Quakers and Methodists, were to oppose this inhuman trade, but many of the city's merchants owned both plantations and slaves, and it was not until the 19th century that links with slavery were severed.

The prosperity of the 18th century made a huge impact on Bristol's architecture. Mansions for wealthy merchants began to spring up, along with handsome Georgian terraces. John Wood the Elder, known as 'Wood of Bath' because of his extensive work in that city, designed the impressive Corn Exchange as a meeting place for Bristol's merchants.

Brunel

In the 19th century the city felt another tremendous influence – that of Isambard Kingdom Brunel. Brunel was not yet 25 years old when his design for a bridge to span the Avon Gorge was accepted. Although the Clifton Suspension Bridge was not completed until after his death, it is his genius that is responsible for this sublime feat of engineering. Many of Brunel's achievements are connected with Bristol. As chief engineer of the Great Western Railway, he planned the line from London to Bristol and designed the first terminus at Temple Meads. He was also responsible for the world's first great ocean-going liners, the ss *Great Western* and the ss *Great Britain*.

Bristol's transformation

Despite the incredible works of Brunel, Bristol began to decline in the 19th century and the once-important port started to lose business to Liverpool and Glasgow. The River Avon has played a central part in Bristol's history: from humble beginnings, through growth and decline as a major port, to recent and on-going regeneration. Its vibrant Harbourside and lively nightlife, coupled with some striking architecture and a rich maritime heritage, prove that Bristol is a true 21st-century city – it has a past but it continues to re-invent itself.

Harbourside

In recent years, Bristol's Harbourside has increasingly become a destination in its own right. It is the focus of major regeneration and development, and has become the cultural and innovative heart of the city. Harbourside is the location for many of Bristol's outstanding museums, galleries and attractions, as well as the Tourist Information Centre.

At-Bristol

At-Bristol

A state-of-the-art interactive science centre, At-Bristol offers an amazing world of hands-on discovery. At-Bristol involves people of all ages in an incredible journey through the workings of the world around us. There is always something new to discover with At-Bristol's programme of special exhibitions, from animation to flight and from illusions to water!

Have you ever wondered how stars are made or how to find the constellations in the night sky? Well, now you can find out. The Planetarium is by the chrome-plated, futuristic sphere in Millennium Square: you can sit back and take a trip to the stars beneath an immersive domed screen in the seasonal star show, just one of many brilliant attractions housed within At-Bristol.

Bristol Aquarium

Embark on a fascinating journey from the British coast through warmer waters to exotic tropical seas. Highlights include a life-size recreation of a sunken ship, a Bristol harbour scene and a wooden footbridge over the open-top giant coral seas display, which are home to sea creatures including sharks and stingrays.

Mshed

Opened in 2011, Mshed is an exciting history museum that tells the story of the city from prehistoric times to the 21st century. Thought-provoking and fun, the museum challenges the perceptions of what it has meant to live in Bristol over the centuries, through the recollections of the people who have shaped the city. There are also working exhibits on the quayside, including steam trains, boats and cranes.

Watershed

Bristol's Harbourside has bars, cafés, museums, shops and two superb art and media centres. One of these is the Watershed which has an excellent reputation as an art-house cinema, and for film education and training. The relaxing and friendly café bar is a popular meeting place.

Bristol Aquarium

Arnolfini

The Arnolfini gallery, café and bar is one of Europe's leading centres for the contemporary arts, all housed in a converted warehouse idyllically situated in the heart of the Harbourside. It also contains one of the country's best arts bookshops. The café bar has quayside seating – a fantastic place to relax al fresco in the summer.

Spike Island

Spike Island is an artspace for the production and exhibition of contemporary art and design, situated on the southern end of Bristol's historic docks in a former Brooke Bond tea-packing factory. She offers visitors a year-round programme of exhibitions, events and family activities in the stunning central gallery spaces. In addition it provides artists' studios and commercial workspace for both new and established designers and creative businesses.

Mshed

Brunel's ss Great Britain

Animation and film

As the home of Aardman Animations characters Wallace and Gromit, Bristol is at the forefront of animation in the UK. The Watershed is the venue for Encounters Film Festival, which is a world-recognized short-film festival held each year. The city's connections with the film industry do not end there – a bronze statue of Bristol-born actor Cary Grant stands in nearby Millennium Square.

Brunel's ss *Great Britain* and the *Matthew*

In 1837, Isambard Kingdom Brunel built the largest ship ever, the ss *Great Western*. His next triumph in 1843 was to be even more influential. Brunel's ss *Great Britain* was the first iron-hulled propeller-driven steamship in the world, making journeys to America and Australia much quicker and more reliable. As the first luxury ocean liner Brunel's ss *Great Britain* set the precedent for ships in the modern age. In her lifetime, the *Great Britain* sailed over a million miles and carried over 15,000 emigrants to Australia. It is fitting that this iron and steel monument to Brunel's genius should have a place in Bristol's future as well as its past, and can be visited in the original Great Western Dock in which she was built over 150 years ago.

A multi award-winning visitor attraction, the ship has been beautifully restored. She offers the chance to travel back in time, and discover true stories of its Victorian passengers and their lives on the two-month voyages. Explore under the water, below the 'amazing glass sea' and investigate the Riggers' Yard.

In the 15th century Henry VII commissioned John Cabot to find unknown lands and the *Matthew* was the ship in which Cabot sailed from Bristol to Newfoundland. A replica of the ship is moored in Bristol, and in 1997 re-enacted Cabot's historic sea crossing.

Up and down the river

For a unique view of the Harbourside – and further afield – visitors can take a leisurely boat ride. There are waterbus and round-trip services, with landing stages which include Temple Meads railway station, Brunel's ss *Great Britain* and Hotwells. In addition there are boat trips around the harbour and special excursions on the River Avon, stopping along the route for pub lunches or picnics.

Watershed

The Harbourside

Clifton and Hotwells

Towards the end of the 18th century Bristol's prosperity grew. Fashionable new housing began to be built on the higher ground above the city and there was renewed interest in the prospect of a bridge over the River Avon. The first design was an ornate five-tiered stone bridge, presented in 1793. Later it was realized that a stone bridge would be prohibitively expensive and so it was for an iron suspension bridge that a competition was run in 1829.

Clifton Suspension Bridge

There were 22 entries, all of which were rejected. The renowned civil engineer Thomas Telford had been called in to judge and, when he submitted his own design, it was accepted. This decision was, perhaps unsurprisingly, unpopular with both other competitors and the public in general.

Another competition, held in 1830, originally had W. Hawks as the winner – just ahead of Brunel, who had submitted four designs. Brunel fought his corner and the judges relented; the decision was reversed and Brunel's 'Egyptian thing' was declared the winner.

Although the first stone was laid in 1831, the bridge was to suffer many years of stop-start production due to the economic climate, the 1831 Bristol riots (over Bristol's meagre representation in Parliament) and, eventually, lack of funds. Ironically, it was Brunel's death in 1859 which led to work restarting. Fellow engineers saw that completing his first serious commission – 'My first child, my darling' – would be a fitting testament to the great man. Brunel's 'darling' was finally opened in a grand ceremony on 8 December 1864.

William Vick was a wine merchant who, when he died in 1754, left an unusual legacy: £1,000 was to be invested and when it grew to £10,000, was to be spent on building a stone bridge across the Avon Gorge. One hundred and ten years would pass before Vick's dream would become the reality that is Bristol's finest landmark, the Clifton Suspension Bridge. For cars there is a toll to cross, but pedestrians and cyclists go free.

Clifton Suspension Bridge

Royal York Crescent

The Downs at Clifton

Clifton Observatory, Camera Obscura and Ghyston's Cave

The Observatory sits high up on the Downs and offers superb views from above the Clifton Suspension Bridge. It is, in fact, one of only two camera obscuras still open to the public in England, and was originally a snuff mill, built by James Waters. William West cut an underground passage to Ghyston's Cave, which was originally only accessible via the cliff face. At the cave mouth, visitors can enjoy spectacular views of the Clifton Suspension Bridge and Avon Gorge below.

Clifton Village and Hotwells

Towards the end of the 18th century Hotwells became known as a fashionable spa. This, combined with the desire of the newly rich to move out of the city into more rarefied air, resulted in extensive building on the slopes above Bristol. Merchants and plantation owners built imposing mansions and elegant terraces, and to this day Clifton Village is still one of Bristol's most exclusive addresses. The magnificent suspension bridge can be seen clearly from Sion Hill, where the zigzag path leads from the Avon Gorge Hotel down to Hotwells. From near the hotel, traces of the Victorian funicular Clifton Rocks Railway can still be glimpsed. In its day, the railway was a tremendous tourist

Clifton Suspension Bridge Visitor Centre

A visitor centre on the Leigh Woods side of the bridge contains displays and artefacts explaining the history, construction and maintenance of this world-famous symbol of the city of Bristol. There is also a retail area that has postcards, greetings cards, information and souvenirs of the Clifton Suspension Bridge.

The Grain Barge at Hotwells

Durdham Downs

attraction: on one day in 1913 it carried over 14,000 people. A volunteer group has been formed to restore elements of the railway, with support from the Avon Gorge Hotel, Bristol City Council and a number of local businesses.

Clifton's best-known address is Royal York Crescent, whose pretty pastel town houses comprise the longest terrace in England and the longest of its type in Europe. To the north of the crescent lie Princess Victoria Street and The Mall, two of Clifton Village's principal shopping streets – where there are shops for exclusive gifts and markets with a bit of everything!

Victorian Clifton

In Victorian times, Bristol developed to the north of Clifton Village. The highlights of Clifton include the Downs, Bristol Zoo Gardens, Clifton College and Bristol's Roman Catholic Cathedral, a startlingly modern building with a light and pleasing interior.

Bristol Zoo Gardens

One of Bristol's most popular attractions, Bristol Zoo Gardens is a conservation charity and has over 400 species of diverse wildlife. The zoo celebrated its 175th anniversary in 2011, and is one of the oldest zoos in the world. Visitors can say hello to the family of gorillas, stroll through the tropical Butterfly Forest or become immersed underwater in the impressive Seal and Penguin Coast. Other zoo favourites include Monkey Jungle, the Reptile House, Asiatic Lions, Bug World, Twilight World and the Aquarium. More adventurous visitors can try the aerial ropes course, Zooropia, to swing alongside some of the zoo's most popular animals, such as gibbons and gorillas, before flying down the zip wire.

The Downs

Clifton is also the point at which the city meets the Downs. Often called 'Bristol's green lung', the Downs stretch from the Avon Gorge to the northern suburbs and are a favourite spot for recreation and relaxation.

Whiteladies Road

One of Bristol's highlights is its vibrant nightlife. In recent years, Whiteladies Road, or the 'strip', has become particularly well-known for its wealth of bars, cafés, pubs and restaurants. Whether you favour African, Italian, Thai, Mexican or British cuisine, Whiteladies Road has an eatery for you.

Bristol Zoo Gardens

Royal West of England Academy

Housed in a Grade II-listed building at the junction of Whiteladies Road and Queen's Road is the Royal West of England Academy. With a permanent collection and temporary exhibitions in various media, it is a leading venue for the fine arts.

Secret Clifton

A walk around the charming neighbourhood of Clifton is a treat. The energetic should consider taking in Windsor Terrace, with its spectacular situation above the Avon Gorge, and The Polygon, a steep and well-kept secret (see pages 10–11 for map).

Balconies in Clifton

The Primrose Café, Clifton

Queen Square

The clock and quarterjacks at Christ Church

St Nicholas Market

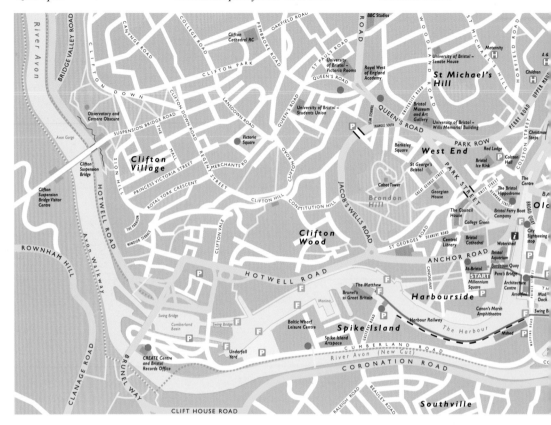

A Walk Around the Old City

Starting at Millennium Square by the **At-Bristol** (page 2) complex, head out of Anchor Square towards the harbour and cross **Pero's Bridge**. This 'horned' footbridge commemorates Pero, an African slave, who was transported from the Caribbean island of Nevis in 1783 and worked for the Pinney family (**see page 16**). Turn right and walk to the **Arnolfini (page 3)** with the statue of **John Cabot** outside. From here you can enjoy a good view of the harbour, Mshed and St Mary Redcliffe church.

Pubs and press-ganging

Walk around the Arnolfini to Prince Street, cross over just before the Bristol Hotel, and enter **Queen Square**. This is one of the earliest and largest squares in England. In the south-east corner is the **Hole in the Wall** pub, whose name derives from the spy-holes that were positioned to watch for press-ganging (taking men by

force for the navy). The pub is thought to be the inspiration behind the Spyglass Inn in R.L. Stevenson's *Treasure Island*.

At the statue of **William III** in the centre of Queen Square head north and go up King William Avenue, turning right into **King Street**. Historic buildings include the **Merchant Venturers' Almshouses** for retired seamen, the **Old Library**, haunts of the poets Coleridge and Southey, the **Bristol Old Vic** theatre and two pubs, **The Old Duke** and **Llandoger Trow**.

The floating harbour

The market and the medieval centre

Walk to the northern end of Welsh Back and turn left across Baldwin Street to climb the steps up to **St Nicholas Street.** Enter the **St Nicholas Market** and walk through to **Corn Street (page 13)**, where the architecture reflects the fact that, by the 18th century, Bristol was one of the most prosperous cities in the country.

Turn right from the **Nails (page 13)** to the junction of **Broad Street**, **Wine Street** and **High Street**, the historic heart of **the old city (page 12)**. Romantic poet Robert Southey was born at 9 Wine Street and Joseph Cottle, his publisher, once had a bookshop on the corner of High Street and Corn Street.

Historic Broad Street

Turn left into Broad Street and you will see **Christ Church** which has 18th-century quarterjacks (figures swinging their hammers against bells on the quarter hour) – as a boy, Robert Southey, who was baptized here, used to stop and watch these. Further down on the right-hand side is the surprisingly colourful ceramic-tiled frontage to the **Edward Everard Printing House**, which depicts Johannes Gutenberg and William Morris. Broad Street ends with the church of **St John the Baptist**. The church tower and spire rise above the surviving medieval gateway, which shows Brennus and Belinus, the city's legendary founders.

Ancient port

Towards the end of King Street, before you cross Queen Charlotte Street, look to the right to see **The Granary**, an example of the Bristol Byzantine style. Walk alongside the timber-framed Llandoger Trow and turn left out of King Street into **Welsh Back.** This was part of the medieval port, before the route of the river was diverted along St Augustine's Reach. The name derives from the Welsh traders who did business with the port in those days.

Along the waterfront

Retrace your steps to the junction of Broad Street and High Street and, turning right, walk towards and across **Bristol Bridge**. Go down the steps on the right and follow the walkway along the waterfront to Redcliffe Bridge. If you wish to make a detour to visit **St Mary Redcliffe (page 14)**, turn left and you will see the church at the roundabout ahead. Otherwise, cross the road to **Redcliffe Wharf**. Follow the waterside path past the entrance to the **Redcliffe Caves** and around the picturesque **Bathurst Basin**, part of Bristol's **floating harbour.** This was constructed in the early 19th century to address the problem of the River Avon's massive tides. The water was diverted along the **New Cut** to the south and was connected to the harbour by a series of locks. Continue along the side of the harbour across Wapping Road. **Mshed (page 2)** is on the left. Further along the harbour is **Brunel's ss *Great Britain* (page 4)**. The replica ship the *Matthew* (**page 4**)can often be seen moored there too.

The Old City

From Saxon times the settlement of Brigstow grew in the area around the confluence of the rivers Frome and Avon. The first bridge across the Avon, where Bristol Bridge is now, would have been made of wood. A later, medieval bridge was made of stone and lined with houses and shops. The town grew in importance in Norman times and a castle was built here. Castle Park, a green area with a waterside walkway, is all that reminds the city of its once-important fortification The city continued to grow, with this medieval centre at its heart; unfortunately many of the city buildings and the docks were bombed during the Second World War in the Blitz of 1940–41. However, there is much in the Old City quarter that does survive from times past.

Bristol Cathedral

Founded as the abbey of St Augustine in the 12th century, this was declared to be a cathedral in 1542, following the Dissolution of the Monasteries. The earliest remaining parts of the cathedral are the abbey gatehouse and the Norman chapter house, the latter being adorned with zigzag decoration and blank arches. The eastern section of the building is very unusual: the aisles, nave and choir stalls rise to the same height. For this reason, the cathedral is one of the foremost examples of a 'hall church' in the country and, indeed, the world. The nave – still unfinished when it was demolished in 1539 – was rebuilt in Victorian times to the medieval design with the original pillar bases, so the cathedral appears much as the medieval abbey would have done.

Bristol Cathedral

Corn Exchange and St Nicholas Market

The junction of Broad Street, Wine Street and High Street is the historic heart of the medieval city while the St Nicholas quarter is famed for its markets. The classical Corn Exchange was designed by John Wood the Elder and highlights the new-found wealth of Georgian Bristol. Merchants used to strike deals on the four Nails outside the Corn Exchange. The expression 'to pay on the nail' derives from this practice. The Corn Exchange is now home to market stalls, selling a range of goods from antiques to computer games and household goods. The Glass Arcade offers more traditional market fare, such as fresh fruit and vegetables, fine foods, flowers and jewellery. There has been a market on the site of the St Nicholas Covered Market since 1743 and still is to this day.

Theatre Royal

Entertainment

King Street is famous for its music, drama and public houses. The Old Duke pub is well-known as a nightly jazz venue, while the timber-framed Llandoger Trow has a fascinating medieval interior. The Theatre Royal, which opened in 1766, is the oldest theatre in the country still working and is home to the famous Bristol Old Vic theatre company.

St Nicholas Market

Castle Park

Redcliffe and Temple

The Redcliffe and Temple areas of Bristol were not, at first, part of Bristol at all. There was a clear divide between the north and south of the River Avon: Redcliffe and Temple lie to the south and were, until the 14th century, administered independently.

St Mary Redcliffe Church

In the Middle Ages the trade in woollen cloth was very important to the southern parishes and the huge wealth of the merchant family, the Canynges, was central to the building of the church.

This cathedral-like church is a noble example of perpendicular architecture. It has a tall spire, transepts and flying buttresses, and inside the piers to the nave ascend beautifully to the gold-embossed vault. William Canynges died before the rebuilding was complete, but he is commemorated in the church by two tombs. Only a few days after his wife's death, he turned his back on commerce and entered the priesthood – so on one tomb he is dressed as a mayor and on the other as a priest.

The birthplace of the 18th-century poet Thomas Chatterton is opposite the church, across Redcliffe Way. Chatterton was born and grew up in

Redcliffe Wharf

Temple Church

The nave, St Mary Redcliffe

Redcliffe but left to seek success in London. Sadly, the literary fame he craved evaded him. At the age of just 17 he was found on his bed, a phial of arsenic by his side. The Pre-Raphaelite artist Henry Wallis depicted the tragedy in his painting *The Death of Chatterton*.

Temple Church

Temple Church was built by the Knights Templar, the soldier-monks from the time of the Crusades, on land across the Avon from Bristol given by Robert, Earl of Gloucester in the mid 12th century. The first church was circular and only its foundations exist. The earliest part surviving today is from the 14th century, although most of the remains date from the 15th century. The dramatic westward lean of the tower, however, developed within a short time of its construction, due to being built on marshy land. The foundations were strengthened and a further section added to the tower, which leans in a different direction from the rest. Temple was a large church with several chantries, including a Weavers' Chapel containing much painted glass. The church was bombed during the Second World War and afterwards was deconsecrated.

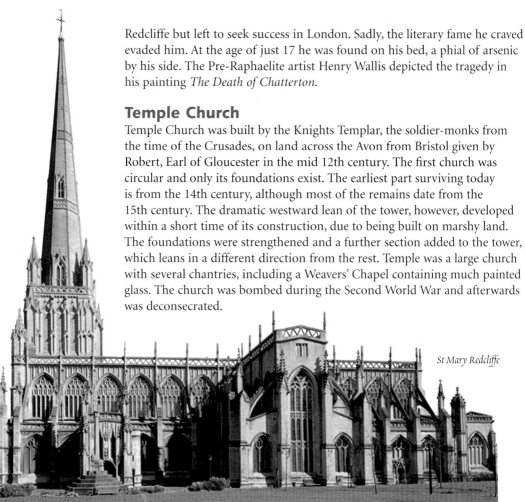

St Mary Redcliffe

The West End

Shopping and restaurants

Shopaholics are well served in Bristol, where the city centre shopping area has over 500 stores. Those who are looking for something a bit different or more contemporary will find what they need in the city's very own West End around Queens Road and Park Street. There is a wide selection of quality shops with clothes outlets from designer to indie, as well as bookshops, and stores specializing in furniture and crafts. In addition to its reputation as a shopping mecca, the West End has some excellent restaurants.

Bristol Museum and Art Gallery

The West End is also something of a cultural hot spot, being home to Bristol Museum and Art Gallery, as well as two of its branch museums, the Georgian House and Red Lodge. These are all free and have much to offer visitors. The main museum has a large collection of decorative and fine art, sculpture, glass, ceramics and many geological exhibits. There are also exciting and ever-changing large exhibitions.

The Georgian House

Built in 1791 for John Pinney, an affluent sugar merchant, this museum has been furnished to provide a fascinating insight into the style of the period. The display depicts life 'upstairs' and 'downstairs'; Pinney owned property and slaves in the West Indies, and the differences between his family's lifestyle and that of their servants are well illustrated.

Red Lodge

This Tudor house was built around 1590 and is now the last surviving Elizabethan interior in Bristol. With exquisite oak panelling, ornate plasterwork ceilings and an impressive stone chimneypiece, Red Lodge is complemented by the restored knot garden outside.

Bristol Museum and Art Gallery, with the Wills Memorial Building, and Bristol University

Red Lodge

The Bristol Hippodrome

This is one of the country's top family-friendly provincial theatres, which proudly continues to stage major West End and Broadway productions.

The Bristol Hippodrome caters for all: whether you prefer musicals, ballet, opera, concerts, comedians or children's shows, the venue's busy programme is almost sure to have something to suit every taste and preference.

Colston Hall

Today, Bristol's largest concert hall presents entertainment by major names in pop and rock music, classical music, stand-up comedy and light entertainment, as well as performances by local choirs, orchestras and schools. Patrons can enjoy a drink or something to eat in the bars or on the roof terrace.

Colston Hall

University of Bristol and Wills Memorial Building

Park Street ascends to the impressive Gothic-style Wills Memorial Building of Bristol University. The Wills family, who were tobacco magnates, provided a large sum of money to help the formal foundation of the university and continued to donate over many years.

Bristol University was founded in 1876 as University College, Bristol, and is proud of its status as the first English higher education institution to admit women on an equal footing to men. It has an excellent international reputation and, commanding a central position as it does, is very much part of the city.

Park Street

Bristol City Centre

Bristol's city centre shopping area is a large and varied destination for shoppers, with a great selection of surprising historical gems mixed in.

Bristol's city centre shopping area

Bristol is one of the UK's top ten shopping destinations. Easily accessible with affordable parking for shoppers, Bristol city centre offers the biggest and best choice of shopping in the south-west. High-end fashion and great value go hand-in-hand, and there's a superb choice of cafés, restaurants and cinemas in which to relax, refuel and be entertained, all within a short stroll of the city's principal attractions and sights. The pedestrianized streets offer a great environment in which to shop and there are many relaxing open spaces in which to watch the world go by.

Cabot Circus is a large, three-tiered shopping and leisure centre, which provides city centre visitors with over 120 shops, including 15 major flagship stores and space for all the high street popular names. Film lovers are spoilt for choice with the arrival of the UK's third Showcase Cinema de Luxe offering 13 screens (four of which show films in 3D), luxurious seating and an exclusive Directors' Lounge. This incredible development in

Shopping at Cabot Circus

City centre shopping

Christmas Steps

the heart of Bristol is covered by a unique shell-shaped glass roof, the only one of its kind in Europe. It is linked by a specially designed raised footbridge to a state-of-the-art car park, allowing visitors to cross Bond Street without having to navigate the traffic below.

Located in the heart of Bristol alongside Cabot Circus is The Galleries, an attractive, three-storey shopping centre, which is home to a further 100 stores. The centre boasts a safe, modern car park with 1,000 spaces, all with special shopper tariffs. A 17th-century enclave of specialist shops can be found nearby at Christmas Steps, between Colston Street and Lewins Mead.

John Wesley's Chapel/The New Room

The chapel is located in the heart of the main shopping area. In 1738, at a meeting in London, John Wesley experienced an assurance of salvation and was determined to bring the same belief to other people. Many clerics were alarmed by his fervency and, coming to Bristol in 1739, Wesley was forced to preach in the open air. He was tremendously successful and 'our New Room in The Horsefair' was built to satisfy the response.

The New Room is the oldest Methodist chapel in the world and it has survived remarkably well. Wesley preached from a double-decker pulpit that is illuminated by a central dome and he stayed – with his brother Charles and other Methodist preachers – in the living quarters above.

John Wesley

Quakers' Friars

Just a few minutes walk from Wesley's chapel is another historical site of non conformism. As early as the 1650s, Quaker meetings were held in a house in Broadmead. After 1669 they were held in Quakers' Friars, in what had been a 13th-century Dominican friary. Today the Quakers' Friars area is a modern piazza, with shops, cafés and restaurants.

Information

Bristol Tourist Information Centre

A good place to begin a visit to any part of the city is the Tourist Information Centre. Set in a spacious location next to the Watershed, with masses of leaflets, information, gifts and helpful, knowledgeable staff, this is also the starting point for Blue Badge guided walks. There is a wide variety of walks offering a great way to find out about Bristol's history, including a chance to join Pirate Pete for an entertaining one-hour walk around the harbour, as he recounts tales of Blackbeard and the city's fascinating maritime past.

Special events:

Bristol Harbour Festival

The Harbour Festival is Bristol's largest, liveliest and most diverse free event, and one of the biggest of its kind in the country. Running annually for over 40 years, the festival and the harbour are animated with dragon boat races, music, dance, strolling entertainment – and much, much more. See www.bristolharbourfestival.co.uk/

St Paul's African Caribbean Festival

Bristol International Balloon Fiesta

Bristol is very much a festival city. Of the numerous special events held throughout the year, the largest and most spectacular is the International Balloon Fiesta. Thousands of visitors come to see the multitude of colourful balloons amidst the glorious parkland of Ashton Court estate, just to the west of the city. The traditional opening ceremony is the 'night glow', when the balloons are tethered and lit up by the flames of their burners, accompanied by music. See www.bristolballoonfiesta.co.uk

'Night glow', Bristol International Balloon Festival

Bristol's BIG Green Week

Bristol's leading reputation as a green city takes centre stage in June with a festival of sustainable development. Bristol's BIG Green Week has a packed schedule of world-class speakers, art, entertainment and family fun with a focus on wildlife. Hosted by various venues in the city, the festival attracts visitors from across the UK and virtual participants from across the world. See www.biggreenweek.com

Cycling in Bristol

Bristol is the hub of Britain's national cycle routes and home to Sustrans, Britain's leading sustainable transport charity. It is no wonder that Bristol has been crowned the UK's first Cycling City, acknowledging the city's growing status as one of Europe's most bike-friendly destinations. Bristol has cycle routes on almost all its major roads, and there are plenty of places to lock up your bike, too. If you are cycling in and around Bristol, be sure to visit the Mud Dock Café Bar on the Harbourside, a unique cycling-themed café. For detailed maps of cycling routes in and around Bristol go to www.sustrans.org.uk